Abstinence Beats Recovery

A compilation of true stories provided by Alcoholics and Drug Addicts about how they got started and the consequences they have suffered. A book written to warn students of the perils of addiciton.

Let's Change the World

A process for becoming a co-worker with Christ to Change the World. Matthew 28:18-20 is your mandate to go and make Disciples of Christ of all nations and Jesus will always be with you.

Let's Change Your Church

A process for becoming a co-worker with Christ to change your church into an Obedience Driven Church. Your church's mission is to change the world.

Let's Change Your School

A process for students to become co-workers with Christ to Change their schools and start a sustained global Christian Discipleship Movement.

Let's Change You

A process for sharing Christ's yoke, to be transformed, and start a sustained, global Christian Discipleship Movement.

Let's Change Your Thinking About Sex and Marriage

How parents and the church must train children about God's reason for sex. Godly sex must be taught from early childhood through marriage.

LET'S CHANGE YOUR SCHOOL

A process for becoming a co-worker with Christ to Change Your School and start a sustained global Christian Discipleship Movement

John and Dot Overton

Edited by: Will Overton
May 2018

www.equippingstudents.com

WESTBOW
PRESS®
A DIVISION OF THOMAS NELSON
& ZONDERVAN

WestBow Press books may be ordered through booksellers or by contacting:

WestBow Press
A Division of Thomas Nelson & Zondervan
1663 Liberty Drive
Bloomington, IN 47403
www.westbowpress.com
1 (866) 928-1240

ISBN: 978-1-9736-3215-3 (sc)
ISBN: 978-1-9736-3216-0 (e)

Library of Congress Control Number: 2018907485

Print information available on the last page.

WestBow Press rev. date: 6/26/2018

Dedication

To the many concerned parents, ministers, and school administrators who are frustrated at how the culture has more influence over their children, youth, and students than they do.

Acknowledgment

Statistical data and Christian classifications have been used from the Barna Group www.Barna.org/research.

The seven checkpoints from Dr. Andy Stanley's book of the same name have been used in our equipping parents, and equipping students processes. Stanley's book focuses on discipling students.

Author's Introduction

We are concerned about our culture and the decline of safety and moral and ethical practices since our school days. There are many contributors to our current condition. We will, however, identify specific ways you can be a vital agent to Change the World by overcoming evil with good on your campuses.

This book focuses on school(s) in your area because the Mosaics/ Millennials (ages 13 through 29) are the future of Christianity and are poorly equipped to cope with the evil and temptations with which our culture surrounds them. Though seemingly unlimited funds are being spent, school shootings, bullying, easy access to tempting drugs and alcohol, perverted sex, and failure to build good and lasting relationships have too often become the norm.

Students make the best change agents on their campuses. It will only take a few committed Christian students to start a sustained spiritual revolution that will spread to other campuses and around the world.

An adult Christian couple (you and your spouse?) should first complete Phase I, Curriculum for Christlikeness from our book, *Let's Change the World,* before attempting to change your school. You then should recruit helpers by teaching Phase II, Equipping Parents (EP) to up to three married couples, or teach Phase III, Equipping Students (ES) to up to six students using the discipleship course described in this book. Throughout this book, you will be referred to as the ES manager or ES teacher.

We have placed Obedience Assignments throughout the following pages. Their purpose is to have your students convert information into action or obedience steps in preparation to change their school(s). A separate student workbook containing these same obedience assignments is available for free downloading from our website, www.equippingstudents.com.

Obedience Assignment: ☐

> 1. Write the purpose of your life.

Check the box after completing the assignment.

"For I know the plans I have for you" declares the Lord, "plans to prosper you, and not to harm you, plans to give you hope and a future" (Jeremiah 29:11).

Why Schools?

Students are the largest unreached people groups in your community. They are making decisions that determine their adult lives and setting their eternal destinies. Unlike schools of the past, today's schools limit themselves to imparting information to students rather than mentoring them in proper relationships.

Our target reader audience is parents of elementary school through college age students. If you agree to become an ES Manager or ES teacher, we will supply you with a companion set of PowerPoint training slides and student manuals from our website www.equippingstudents.com.

Alternatively, upon request, we will deliver a thumb drive to you with all of the materials needed to recruit helpers and disciple students.

All students are spiritual beings living in temporary physical bodies. The following pages are a summarized discipleship course for students and we will focus on seven training topics as supplements to their scholastic training. These training topics are specific disciplines for students to practice. The topics from Dr. Stanley's book, The Seven Checkpoints are: 1) Authentic Faith or Know your purpose, 2) Spiritual Disciplines, 3) Moral boundaries, 4) Healthy friendships, 5) Wise Choices, 6) Ultimate Authority, and 7) Others First. We call the process of applying these topics, Equipping Students (ES).

The first ES session is the most important of all. The teacher(s) and the students need to become well acquainted and transparent with each other.

The session is designed to make sure your students are not just religious but are true Christians. You should camp here until the group has demonstrated that their faith in Christ is indeed authentic.

The commitment expected of each student must be clearly understood and agreed upon. If they commit to eight one and a half hour discipleship sessions, and to be accountable for accomplishing weekly goals, they will be presented with a Study Bible, and an ES binder with student manuals, journal, and pen. They will need to bring their ES binder and pen to all ES sessions.

The remainder of this book will be written to students that you will disciple.

Student Session #1

Authentic Faith - (Know Your Purpose)

Never lose sight of your ES objective, which is to be equipped by knowing your purpose as a Disciple of Christ that will take the Gospel onto your campus(es). The strategy

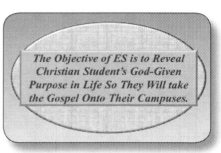

The Objective of ES is to Reveal Christian Student's God-Given Purpose in Life So They Will take the Gospel Onto Their Campuses.

will be to join a group of no more than five other students that will become Disciples of Christ and start a sustained global spiritual revolution. Proverbs 3:5-6, "Seek God's will in all you do, and He will show you the path (Purpose) of life". This will be the theme for your entire ES discipleship course.

You may bring your study Bible to each class or you may prefer to use your smart phone or tablet if available. Always bring your binder, journal, and pen.

Each session has six parts. Power point presentations are available for each session and student manuals following the presentations are in your binders.

1. Opening Prayer:

An adult teacher will facilitate each ES session. Student must realize that they are being held accountable for the ES process and assistance to the teacher will be expected. The teacher will lead in the first session opening prayer and students will assist in opening all future sessions. The focus of the prayers will be on your schools and your group's spiritual growth. Specifically pray for the students of your school(s), teachers, parents, administrators, cooks, janitors, etc.

The teacher will serve as an encourager to assure you about your life purpose. They will either rotate the opening amongst the group or ask more than one to pray. All should realize that this is part of your training. Public prayer may be awkward for some initially, but this is your learning laboratory.

You will be encouraged to spend time with Jesus in prayer each day.

2. How Are You Doing Spiritually?

The teacher will lead in this part of Session 1 by sharing his/her relationship with Jesus. Then each student will be asked to share their relationship with Jesus. The teacher will tell about his/her daily Bible study and prayer time. Emphasis must be placed on being brief and honest.

Each student will use form ES1 in your ES binder to write "Your Story."

Obedience Assignment: ☐

> **2. Use Your ES1 form to write your story. Be very brief.**

Your story is your relationship with Jesus. If you are not practicing a daily time with Jesus in prayer and Bible study, use this discipleship course to start.

Keep your story very brief.

Obedience Assignment: ☐

> **3. Locate a Secret Place. Keep your Bible, Journal, and binder there.**

Locate a secret place away from all human sounds. Keep your Bible, Journal, and ES Binder there.

This should be a well-lit, comfortable place of privacy for you.

Take a sabbatical from as many responsibilities as you can to make time to practice the daily disciplines of prayer, study, and journaling in your secret place.

Obedience Assignment: ☐

> **4. Use Your ES1 form to write John 3:16. This is the Good News: The Gospel. Memorize it.**

Also, use form ES2 to list the names of student friends you know that are away from God. Keep your filled out forms in your binder. You may make revisions later.

3. Accountability Time:

The teacher will use the third part of Session 1 to explain to the group about weekly goal setting and follow up accountability.

Examples of goals to accomplish next week will be identified. You should think about your future goals.

You will need a link or bridge between your story and the Gospel.

Obedience Assignment: ☐

> **5. Use Your ES1 form to write a brief bridge from your story to the Gospel (John 3:16).**

You will use one Bible verse to represent the Gospel (Good News). John 3:16 is that verse. Write John 3:16 using ES1 form. Memorize it and repeat it often in your mind.

Obedience Assignment: ☐

6. Use your journal to write why it is important to be accountable for reporting your goals.

Your story, your bridge and John 3:16 must work together to clearly communicate your relationship with Jesus and how that provides you with faith that is authentic, and assurance of your salvation.

Each group member will be assured that they will be expected to share the results of their goals at the following meeting.

Obedience Assignment: ☐

7. Write the goals you expect to accomplish this year.

You will use your journal to write why it is important to be accountable for reporting your goals. Use your journal to write the goals you expect to accomplish this year.

Obedience Assignment: ☐

8. Why do you think Jesus commands you to deny your selfishness?

Use your journal to write ways to not be selfish when with a group of your peers.

4. Vision Casting:

The teacher will make a brief presentation of encouragement and assurance that the members of the group *can* accomplish their goals and bring about a spiritual revolution.

Biblical principles, verses, parables, and illustrations will be used during these times of casting positive vision for the group. Emphasis will be given to John 15:5 (Apart from Christ,

you can do nothing!) and Philippians 4:13 (You can do all things through Christ who strengthens you) during session 1.

The group will be told about how to treat "selfishness."

You are not expected to accomplish great spiritual goals alone but to deny your selfishness and learn to depend upon Christ for your strength.

Jesus said, "I am the True Vine; you are the branches. If you remain in me and I in you, you will bear much fruit, apart from me you can do nothing" (John 15: 5).

The Roman government nailed common criminals to crosses of execution. Though Jesus never broke a civil or moral law, he was falsely accused and executed on a cross. The cross has since become the symbol of Christianity and many wear crosses to show that they are Christ's disciples.

Obedience Assignment: ☐

9. If you do not currently wear a cross, do so as a symbol that you follow Jesus

Be bold in living a Christlike life before your fellow students.

Unlike your culture which promotes a mindset of looking out for yourself above every one else. Do you sense the tension between Jesus' command and pressure from your peers? Do you think that selfishness will interfere with the accomplishment of your life goals?

Obedience Assignment: ☐

> 10. Use your secret place. Make dated journal entries.

Having a secret place is most valuable to becoming a Disciple of Christ. Use it daily.

5. Brief Discipleship Lesson:

The first discipleship lesson will be on Know your Purpose.

Do you know what your life purpose is? If not, would you like to know? The Bible tells us that we can and should know our purpose in life.

You should be preparing now, while you are a student, to fulfill your purpose. You need to prepare for the vocation that will pave the way to fulfill that purpose.

Christianity is a lifestyle rather than a legalistic religion. As long as you hold on to your life for yourself, you will never know your (His) purpose. Jesus said, "He that loses his life for me shall find it." That is, whoever will give up his own life for Jesus' sake will find the purpose for his/her life. It may be expressed as an engineer, pilot, farmer, welder, wife, dad, writer, etc.

True Christian faith is very specific. It is not faith in a moral system, an organization, other people, or a program. It is confidence that Jesus is who He says He is and assurance that He will do everything He has promised to do. Only He reveals a person's purpose for being created.

Authentic Faith is believing that Jesus is the Son of God and His sacrificial death has been accepted by God the Father as payment in full for your sins.

Your purpose is more clearly identified as you advance as a disciple or follower of Jesus.

Care must be given in the way you pray. If you pray to get things from God that He has not promised to provide, then you can become disappointed in God and your faith in Him may falter. A future session on spiritual disciplines will instruct you in the proper way to pray and expect to have your prayers answered.

Your faith must be based specifically upon a relationship with the person: Jesus. Authentic faith requires you to accept what has been promised even though you may not understand it. This is one of the most difficult parts of being an effective Christian since we have been taught in our schools to only trust in those things that we understand.

It helps if you realize that God is infinite and you are not. You are finite and unable to comprehend all spiritual things. You are therefore instructed to not depend upon your understanding but to trust that your infinite Heavenly Father knows what is best for you.

Students are learners preparing themselves for a quality adult life. Learning your purpose in life and how to live with authentic faith is the best preparation you can make for the future.

God promises to direct your life if you trust Him with all of your being.

Growing faith is built upon a process: 1) Gaining truthful knowledge from studying the Bible, 2) Believing what the Bible tells you, and 3) Trusting that God will respond with what He has promised.

Spend time with Jesus daily in your secret place. Determine to trust Jesus with His promises to you.

Study your Bible to learn of His promises. Start with the New Testament book of John. Then return to Matthew, Mark, and Luke.

6. Goal Setting

The final part of Session 1 is to set goals for the upcoming week. The teacher will assure you that he/she promises to also set weekly goals and be prepared to discuss the results at each ES session.

There are six specific goals to be set following the first meeting: 1) Secure a secret place; 2) Practice daily, dated journal entries; 3) Start reading a chapter of the Book of John each day; 4) Add to the list of students you know to be away from God; 5) Revise

your brief story about your relationship with Jesus; and 6) memorize Proverbs 3:5-6.

Obedience Assignment: ☐

11. Memorize Proverbs 3:5-6

"Trust the Lord with all your heart and lean not on your own understanding, acknowledge Him in all your ways and He will direct your paths" (Proverbs 3:5-6).

John and Dot Overton

Obedience Assignment: ☐

> 12. Use your journal to
> write the purpose of ES.

Spend time with Jesus daily in your secret place. Determine to trust Jesus. Ponderwhat your campus can be like when all of your peers are Disciples of Christ. The objective of ES is to reveal Christian student's God-given purpose in life so they will take the Gospel onto their campuses.

Student Session #2

Spiritual Disciplines

Be sure to bring your ES Binder, Journal, and Pen. It will not be necessary to bring your Study Bible unless you just want to.

Starting with the second ES session, you may be appointed to serve as a teacher assistant. The teacher will instruct as well as encourage and coach you as the student assistant.

Obedience Assignment: ☐

1. Opening:

> 13. Use your journal to describe a Disciple of Christ.

The teacher will inform you that prayers for the accomplishment of God's will are always answered. It is God's will that you know your purpose in life and that no one perish.

Leading in opening prayer will be accomplished by students and the focus of the prayers for session 2 will be the identification of additional names of students known to be away from God.

Prayers should include adoration, respect, and love of God your Creator.

Your knowledge of the Bible will be very beneficial in effective prayer.

Each student will also ask to be empowered by the Holy Spirit to complete the entire ES course. Prayers are like voice messages to God. The Father paid for the message by Jesus, His Son.

2. How Are You Doing Spiritually?

The teacher will ask each student to share with the rest of the group how they are doing spiritually. You will be specifically asked to share about your relationship with Jesus. Sharing may have to be limited to only one or two students.

The teacher must be time conscious and not let any one speaker dominate this part of the ES session.

3. Accountability Time:

The teacher will designate specific students to share about their progress with their goals during the past week. You will never be asked for accountability in a way that can be answered by a single word. You will always be prompted to use sentences to share how you accomplished your weekly goals.

The teacher will ask selected students to tell where their secret place is located and have them tell what they learned from the chapter of John that they read this morning. You may use your Journal as a reminder. How many days have you made entries in your Journal? How did you identify students known to be away from God that have been added to your list?

Briefly tell your Story and repeat Proverbs 3:5-6.

4. Vision Casting:

The teacher will assure the group that they *can* make a spiritual impact on their school(s). Basic to the Christian life is the belief that the Bible is the source of Truth and that you should build your life on the foundation of the Bible.

Using your secret place to study the Bible and pray is the way to build your relationship with Jesus, receive the power needed to learn your purpose in life, and accomplish your goals.

The Bible assures you that you are not to attempt your Christian deeds alone; you are empowered by God the Holy Spirit to carry out the commissions and commands that God calls you to do. Acts 1:8 informs us that our Christian influence is to grow beyond ever expanding boundaries.

You are not to become a Christian and wait until you die and go to heaven. You are to have an active life as a co-laborer with Jesus until you die. You will accumulate rewards for eternity.

Too often, you will get discouraged and fail to tell other students your story. That will happen if you do not wait and depend upon being empowered by the Holy Spirit. That is why it is necessary to use your secret place to practice the disciplines of daily Bible study, prayer, and journaling.

The group is to depend upon Christ for their strength. This will require much discipline.

You will learn to use a very simple, three-step process 1.) Telling our story, 2.) Bridging it to the Gospel, and 3.) **Citing** John 3:16 as the Gospel in future sessions.

The Gospel (Good News) can be summed up by a single scripture: John 3:16. Most people know this scripture. Recite it in your mind often.

Regroup into pairs and briefly practice this simple three-step process. Use the Story and Bridge you have written in your ES binder if it will help.

That was simple wasn't it?

Now let us rearrange in different groups of two or three and 1.) Tell your story, 2.) Bridge to the Gospel, and 3.) Recite John 3:16.

This process must be kept simple and easy to remember. Recite the process in your mind often, imagining that you are sharing it with someone on your list of students.

5. Brief Discipleship Lesson:

The second Discipleship lesson will be on Spiritual Disciplines.

You will focus on three Christian disciplines during this coming week:

1) Daily Bible Study,
2) Daily Prayer, and
3) Daily Journaling

Obedience Assignment: ☐

> 14. Use your journal to list some spiritual disciplines.

In your own words, write what you think a Disciple of Christ is and how to become one.

Obedience Assignment: ☐

> 15. Agree with Jesus to practice the three daily disciplines in your secret place: Study, Prayer, and Journaling.

What is the difference between a disciple and discipline?

Write the three spiritual disciplines in your journal being emphasized this week.

6. Goal Setting:

The final part of Session 2 is to set eight goals for the upcoming week: 1) Start using your secret place daily to 2) Continue daily Bible reading (continue with the book of John), 3) Journal and date your impression of the Bible chapter you read, 4) Continue a daily time of prayer, confess any known sins 5) Add to your list of students known to be away from God, 6) Review your brief story about your authentic faith in Jesus, 7) Write your bridge to the Gospel, and 8) Memorize Acts 1:8. "You will receive power when the Holy Spirit comes on you; and you will be my witnesses in Jerusalem, and in all Judea and Samaria, and to the ends of the earth."

Obedience Assignment: ☐

> **16. Memorize Acts 1:8.**

Acts 1:8 assures you of two very important facts about living the Christian life. 1) You will receive power from the Holy Spirit to do what Jesus has told you to do, and 2) You will be a co-laborer with Jesus by witnessing about what He has done in your life to all nations. Meditate on Acts 1:8 and repeat it in your mind.

Student Session #3

Moral Boundaries

By session 3, the group should be aware of their purpose in life and their role as Christian disciples. They will likely still feel inadequate and that is OK because they are in training. Each should be given assistant roles in the conducting of the sessions, though they may resist it and may not do a very good job. Experience is what they need to transform them from being a consumer Christian to being a Disciple of Christ.

A group member will be appointed to be the teacher assistant for this session. The teacher must perform the teaching role and be available to encourage and coach the student assistant(s).

1. Opening:

The student assistant will lead in opening prayer. He/she should decide the format of prayer for the session. Student-led prayer will be the opening for future ES sessions. Prayer emphasis for session three should be for the members of the group and their classmates.

2. How Are You Doing Spiritually?

The teacher will ask each student to share with the rest of the group about how they are doing spiritually. You will be asked to tell about your secret place and how you are using it.

During this important part of session three, the teacher must be alert to keeping the sharing time on topic. Due to the inexperience of the group, it will be very easy to get off the subject. Tactfully reminding those sharing to bring their time to a close is a part of both the teacher and student discipleship training.

3. Accountability Time

The teacher will use this Session 3 time to designate specific students to share with the group about their progress with their goals during the past week. Again, this is part of ES discipleship training.

By session 3, the group members should know that they will be accountable for sharing the results of their goals at the next meeting.

Selected students will be asked:

1) Share some things you journaled this week in your secret place.
2) Which chapters of the Bible are you studying? How do you truly feel about spending time reading the Bible?
3) Share how you met the names you added to your list.

4) Tell how confessing known sins affects your time in prayer.

Obedience Assignment: ☐

> 17. Do you hesitate to confess known sins? (Y) (N)

Do you find it easy to reject certain temptations because you know you will need to confess it again?

5) Quickly recite your story, bridge, and John 3:16.
6) Why do you think John 1:14 says, "The Word became human and dwelt among us?"
7) Recite Acts 1:8.

Obedience Assignment ☐

> 18. Use your journal to list some things you have given up.

What are some things you have given up to make time to study your Bible, pray, and journal daily?

4. Vision Casting:

The teacher will reassure the group that they **can** make a spiritual impact on their school campus. Your attitude determines your accomplishments and failures in life. Having a "Can-Do Attitude" will help you be obedient to Jesus and accomplish great things in His kingdom.

Just because something has not been done before should not be accepted as a reason for not believing it can be done now. All great discoveries are the result of an individual's **Can-Do** Attitude.

Obedience Assignment: ☐

> 19. If you have a fear of failure or rejection, ask Jesus to help you develop a "Can Do" attitude.

The greatest barrier to success is the fear of failure. The hardest part of any voyage is taking the first step.

We all have our limits when we act alone, but we have a promise from the Bible that we can do all things through Christ who will always be with you. You should be developing good friendships with students of the other gender. You *Can Do* it.

5. Brief Discipleship Lesson:

The teachers will lead the third and fourth Discipleship emphasis, which will be on Moral Boundaries. Two adults will teach this discipleship lesson if the class is a mix of boys and girls. During the discipleship lesson, the girls will relocate to a separate room to be instructed by a mature Christian woman while the boys will remain to be instructed by a mature Christian man.

A moral code is a system of morality (according to a particular philosophy, religion, culture, etc.) and a moral is any one practice or teaching within a moral code. An example of a moral is the Golden Rule, which states that, "One should treat others as one would like others to treat you".

Christianity is about proper relationships: your relationship with Jesus, parents, and with other students. Developing proper relations with the other gender must start early in life.

Christian families are designed to teach you proper relationships. Your relationship with your parents starts your proper relationship with God. If you feel that your family has failed you in this regard, you should vow to do better for the next generation.

The Bible is clear about the boundaries that are best for you. Though the culture often teaches otherwise, these boundaries are not set to prevent students from enjoying life. Indeed, they are proclaimed so you can enjoy a quality, free life.

Obedience Assignment: ☐

> 20. Make a mental boundary regarding sex that you will not cross.

Remember, abstinence is far better than trying to recover from bad choices.

We will look at several examples of morals that Disciples of Christ should maintain.

God created and still owns and controls the universe. God has established His rules for the proper operation of His universe. You have been created by Him with a God-given purpose.

Unfortunately, you live in a culture that has grossly perverted the rules God has established for your benefit. Your spiritual enemy, Satan, places temptations in your life to draw you away from your purpose and the quality lifestyle that God has planned for you.

Peer pressure is used to tempt you to cross your God established boundaries. You can be distracted from God's purpose for your life by many things. Unless you practice daily communion with Jesus, you will succumb to selfish distractions.

Girls are more effective in holding to moral boundary lines of life. This especially applies to drugs, alcohol use, and sex.

You have a free will and are able to make good or bad choices. The choices you make now will have long lasting effects such as qualifications for the work force, college, marriage, future families, and eternity.

How far is too far? Where should you draw the line? The farther you go, the faster you go. The further you go, the further you want to go. The further you go, the harder it is to turn back. Where you draw the line will determine a lot about the quality of your future.

Your spiritual enemy will tempt you to cross your moral boundary now to enjoy the immediate pleasures of sin. He fails to inform you of the destructive consequences of not abstaining.

He wants you to join his crowd, and travel the broad road that leads to destruction.

Obedience Assignment: ☐

> 21. Do you agree that morality related to gender is perverted in your school? (Y) (N)

If you observe abuse or harassment amongst your peers, go to the one being bullied and offer your support, encouragement, and friendship.

Remember, abstinence is far better than trying to recover from bad choices.

There is a difference in sex drive following puberty and the female is more inclined to hold the line beyond which she will not cross though peer pressure may suggest otherwise. God's purpose for this physical characteristic is to cause a mutual attraction between males and females for marriage.

Cultural trends regarding sexual behavior are perhaps the strongest temptation on your spiritual enemy's list. Peer pressure can become almost overwhelming, but the rewards for holding the line are well worth it.

6. Goal Setting: The final part of Session 3 is to set goals for the upcoming week. There are six specific goals to be set for the week: 1) Do a good deed for a student of the opposite gender, 2) Continue daily Bible study and dated journaling, 2) Continue a daily time of prayer, 3) Pray specifically for those on your list and for your classmates, 4) Tell your brief story about the results of your faith in Jesus to someone on your list, 5) Meditate on your bridge to the Gospel, and 6) Memorize Philippines 4:13. "I can do all things through Christ who strengthens me".

Obedience Assignment: ☐

22. Memorize Philippians 4:13. Meditate on your bridge to the Gospel and this verse often.

Do not try to stay on the correct side of your sexual boundary alone. Remember that you can do it in Christ who is always with you and strengthens you.

We will continue the discipleship topic of Moral Boundaries at our next meeting.

Student Session #4

Moral Boundaries Cont.

Session 4 is a continuation of Session 3 on the topic of Moral Boundaries. God created sex as a beautiful expression of love between a man and his wife. Satan has perverted sex into a  powerful tool for his purposes: Evil. ES will use two sessions for this most important moral teaching since foundations for future Godly homes will be established by you and your fellow students by practicing abstinence.

You may want to reference our book, Let's Change Your Thinking about Sex and Marriage on our website www.equippingstudents.com

1. Opening:

Opening prayer will be accomplished by one of the students. Ask that the Holy Spirit lead to bold moral lines across which group members will not cross. The format for the Opening of the 4th session will be determined by the student assistant.

2. How Are You Doing Spiritually?

The teacher will choose different group members to share how they are doing spiritually. Students may need to be prompted to share their true feelings about spending daily time in communion with Jesus in their secret place. How is your daily time in your secret place equipping you for the day?

Is the new discipline something you look forward to or do you consider it to be an obligation that you should perform? Can you truthfully say that your personal, quiet time with Jesus is helpful in coping with the issues of your life or not?

Obedience Assignment: ☐

23. Honestly record in your journal your attitude about spending time with Jesus in your secret place

These times of sharing must be honest and truthful, never flavored with statements that sound good just to impress the other group members!

3. Accountability Time:

The teacher will use this Session 4 time to call on different students to share about their progress with their goals during the past week. Remember, accountability questions should always be answered with sentences and the teacher should never accept a one-word answer. This is an important part of the group discipleship training.

1) Share about the good deed you did this past week.
2) Tell about your Secret Place, and how you spend time studying the Bible, journaling, and praying each day.
3) How did the student you shared Your Story with respond?
4) Tell your Story and Bridge to the Gospel.
5) Recite Philippines 4:13, "I can do all things through Christ who strengthens me".

Obedience Assignment: ☐

> 24. Pray for those on your list and for your classmates.

Develop the discipline of praying daily for the students you know that are away from God. Ask Jesus to arrange opportunities for you to speak to them.

4. Vision Casting:

The teacher will reassure each of you that you can make a spiritual impact on your school through the discipline of Self Control. This is one attribute of the Christian life that cannot be concealed.

Your natural inclination is to gratify *Self* and *Self* will dominate you. Radical Jesus instructed you to take up your cross of execution **daily** if you truly want to be His Disciple. Most students have never understood this radical command from Luke 9:23.

You may be a shy student and are reluctant to even talk to a student of the opposite gender.

Obedience Assignment: ☐

> 25. Do a good deed for a student of the opposite gender.

As part of your discipleship training, you should work on developing proper moral relationships with both boys and girls.

Obedience Assignment: ☐

> 26. Why do you think it will help you to do a good deed for someone of the opposite gender?

The best way to enjoy friends is to be friendly to other students. Take the initiative and invite both boys and girls to your home to listen to your music collection or to join you for a coke at a local cafe. Ask them to share their likes and dislikes rather than dominate the conversation. In other words, be a good listener and truly become interested in their lives.

Self has an unquenchable appetite, which will lead a person into all sorts of addictions!

You must depend upon the Holy Spirit daily to be most influential for Christ on your campus. Rather than being selfish, you should display the characteristics (fruit) of the Holy Spirit which is love, joy, peace, patience, kindness, goodness, faithfulness, gentleness, and self control.

Satan's greatest tool to ruin a person's Christlikeness is perverted sex!

Obedience Assignment: ☐

> 27. Enter in your journal the name of a student, of the other gender on your list that you will speak to.

Be a good listener and show real interest in others.

Whereas God's plan is to prepare males and females for genuine intimacy in marriage, Satan's plan is to steal, kill, and destroy the beautiful life God has in store for you by tempting you with instant gratification (John 10:10).

Breakup of the nuclear family (father, mother, children) results in all sorts of cultural dysfunctions, morally and ethically. The church is to counteract such disorder, but she is failing and Christian parents are failing to obey Jesus' instructions for proper family life.

Failure in marriages has become the greatest hindrance to the spread of the Gospel. Satan knows that and starts early in student's lives to pervert what quality family life is intended to be.

Unless you are convinced that self must be dealt with as Jesus instructed (death to self), Satan cleverly and subtly tempts you with addictive habits like sexual perversion to destroy the foundations upon which intimate marriage is intended to be built!

5. Brief Discipleship Lesson:

The fourth Discipleship emphasis will be a continuation on moral boundaries: Sex before Marriage - Self Control.

How far is too far? Where will you draw the line? Where you draw the line is where Satan starts his temptations.

God is not against sex since He created it and He is not against students since He created them as well. God knows it is best for students and the Christian movement to wait until marriage for sexual intimacy.

Sex is for married people because sex is not physical; it is relational. It is to be reserved for the unique, committed, multifaceted relationship of marriage. Only between man and wife can sex be the wonderful and intimate experience that God intends.

God designed sexual attraction between males and females. As students age, this attraction increases and will go through a progression of stages.

Stage 1 students of opposite genders may just enjoy being with each other.

Stage 2 They may advance to showing affection by holding hands. Holding hands will likely advance to Stage 3 in which the boy embraces her by placing his arm around her shoulder and her permitting it.

As this progression continues, it is usually the female that determines where the limit or boundary will be drawn. The male is typically the more aggressive and the female more cautious. She will set the limits as she discerns if his intentions are being expressed because he cares for her rather than using her. Self-control involves the boy and the girl cooperating with each other.

If the relationship continues unchecked, it will likely lead to more intimate contact like kissing. This is natural but must be controlled by both male and female.

6. Goal Setting:

The final part of Session 4 is to set goals for the upcoming week. There are six specific goals to be set following the fourth meeting: 1) Do another good deed for a different student of the opposite gender, 2) Continue a daily Bible study and dated journal, 3) Continue a daily time of prayer, 4) Pray specifically for those on your list and for your classmates, 5) Tell your brief story about the results of your authentic faith in Jesus to someone on your list and Bridge to the Gospel, and 6) Memorize Luke 9:23.

Obedience Assignment: ☐

28. Memorize Luke 9:23   "Whoever wants to be My disciple must deny themselves and take up their cross daily and follow me."

Student Session #5

Healthy Friendships

The direction you take in life will be highly influenced by the friends you keep. For the Christian this is a balancing act between influencing others for Christ and being influenced by others for evil.

The discipleship lesson that is part of session 5 will be taught by an adult teacher and assisted by an appointed student group member. The group will **not** be separated by boys and girls for the remainder of ES.

1. Opening:

The student assistant should lead the opening prayer time. The format for the opening of the 5th session will have each group member present take a few moments to be silent before the Lord and ask His Holy Spirit to energize the meeting.

Each member should pray for the students on their list and ask the Holy Spirit to remind them of additional names that are away from God.

The teacher will close this part of the ES session in prayer.

2. How Are You Doing Spiritually?

The teacher will choose group members that have not shared recently to share how they are doing spiritually. If they hesitate, ask them to share about their times of daily meditations (Bible study, prayer, journaling, etc.) in their secret place and how they are changing spiritually.

3. Accountability Time:

The teacher will use this time to call on different students to share about the progress they made with their goals during the past week.

1) Share about the good deed you did this past week and how the student responded.
2) Tell the group about your time spent studying the Bible, journaling, and praying in your secret place.
3) How have some students responded favorably to Your Story?
4) Recite Luke 9:23; "Whoever wants to be my disciple must deny themselves and take up their cross daily."

Obedience Assignment: ☐

4. Vision Casting:

> 29. Do you want to be a Disciple of Christ? (Y) (N)
> Do you take up your cross daily? (Y) (N)

The teacher will cast a vision for the group about the permanent position they have in Christ. They have been equipped to bring others into the Kingdom. They are holy, blameless, and beyond reproach! Whether they feel like it or not.

Yet He (Christ) has now reconciled you in His fleshly body through death, in order to present you before Him (God) holy and blameless and beyond reproach (Colossians 1: 22).

Jesus has exchanged His righteousness for your sins. Since you are now free from the penalty of your sins and the power of sin, you are commissioned and spiritually equipped to help other students enjoy the same freedom that you enjoy.

Jesus told Peter, a commercial fisherman, that he could become a fisher of men. As one with authentic faith, you too can be a fisher of men (students)! That has got to be the most awesome responsibility anyone can have. Like the fishermen and tax collectors that Jesus chose to be His disciples, He has chosen you, a student, to continue sharing the Good News (Gospel), with those you know who are away from God; your fellow students.

Obedience Assignment: ☐

> 30. Do you sense that you are changing spiritually? (Y) (N) Are you enjoying a closer fellowship with Jesus? (Y) (N)

As a co-laborer with Jesus, you can accomplish great spiritual things on your campus. Become intentional in making friends with the students on your list. Experience the wonderful benefits of having friends with which you can share Jesus.

5. Brief Discipleship Lesson - Healthy Friendships

Your friends are the most influential people in your life. Cultural changes have elevated the role friends play in your life. Influence can be predominately from your friends to you or from you to those you select as friends.

To be an effective fisher of men, you must carefully accept others as your friends rather than reject them.

During the 1960s, polls showed the three most influential factors in a student's life to be 1.) Parents, 2.) Teachers, and 3.) Spiritual leaders.

Today the three most influential factors in a student's life are 1.) Friends, 2.) Media, and 3.) Parents. Spiritual Leaders dropped to 17th!

Acceptance paves the way to influence. When students feel accepted, they drop their guard.

Students resist the influence of those that they feel do not accept them.

6. Goal Setting:

The final part of Session 5 is to set goals for next week.

There are six specific goals to be set following the fifth meeting. 1) Prayerfully review your list of students and add new names as prompted by the Holy Spirit, 2) Share your story with a student that does not appear to have a friend, 3) Tell them about ES and ask if they would be interested in joining an ES group, 4) Eat lunch with a student that is sitting alone, 5) Select an entry in your Journal to share with the group, and 6) Memorize Matthew 4:19.

Obedience Assignment: ☐

31. Memorize Matthew 4:19

Jesus said, "Follow Me and I'll make you Fishers of Men."

Make an all out effort to spot a student that is eating alone. Ask to sit with them and ask about the courses they are taking and ask about their future plans.

Obedience Assignment: ☐

32. Eat lunch with a student that is eating alone.

Be alert to an opportunity to tell them that you are looking to make new friends and ask if they would like to be friends.

Obedience Assignment: ☐

33. Tell your story to a student that does not seem to have a friend. Tell him/her that you would like to be their friend.

If you receive a favorable response, tell him/her about your ES group.

Ask if they would be interested in learning more about ES

Obedience Assignment: ☐

> 34. Tell your new friend about ES and ask if they would be interested in joining an ES group.

If they show an interest in ES, turn their name into your ES teacher as a candidate for a future group.

Explain that a commitment must be made to be accepted into an ES group and that they will be held accountable for accomplishing weekly goals.

Student Session #6

Wise Choices

We all must make choices and our choices chart the course of our future, especially our eternal future!

The ES teacher will serve as the primary instructor for this ES Session. A student assistant will be selected to help as part of their training.

1. Opening:

Freedom is Not Free! Someone paid a high price for your freedom.

Others have made choices that you might consider unwise, but their choices have led to your benefit: We Are Free!

The ES group should bow, close their eyes, and be silent for a few moments just thinking about what military men of the past have endured (even died) in order to protect them and provide them with a free country. Then allow their minds to focus on what Jesus did to provide us freedom from the penalty of our sins and from the power of sin.

- Being Abandoned
- Being Rejected

- Being Disappointed
- Being Falsely Accused
- Being Abused
- Being Tortured
- Being Executed as a common criminal
- Having the sins of the world (including all of the sins of the group) put on Him
- Having The Father Forsake Him

Living in a free country is wonderful but having eternal life with Christ is absolutely amazing!

The teacher will close this part of the ES session with prayer.

2. How Are You Doing Spiritually?

The teacher will choose different group members to share how they are doing spiritually.

By ES session six, each group member should be accustomed to speaking openly about his or her spiritual walk with Jesus. If there are times of silence, the teacher should refer to his/her ES manual and prompt the student being called upon to speak about some of the previous sessions.

Are you and Jesus acquainted? Using your secret place to meet with Jesus daily should establish a close fellowship with Him. More important than knowing Jesus is assurance that He knows you. It is urgent that you spend daily time in your secret place in communion with Him (Matthew 7:23).

3. Accountability Time:

The teacher will use this time to call on different students to share the progress they made with their goals during the past week.

1) Share about your offer to have lunch with a student eating alone this past week and how they responded. Are they interested in taking a future ES Course?
2) Share some specific ways you pray for those on your list. How many are now on your list?
3) Briefly share one of your Journal entries.
4) How has adjusting your attitude toward others made you more attractive to students that needs friends?
5) Recite Matthew 4:19; Follow me, and I will make you fishers of men."

Obedience Assignment: ☐

4. Vision Casting:

35. What does it mean to be a fisher of men?

The teacher will cast a vision for the group about the call to be a visionary Disciple of Christ.

According to the Biblical teaching of Jesus, God the Father loves everyone and wants none to perish but for all to enjoy eternal life with Him. The alternative to eternal life with the Father is eternal death separated from Him in a horrible place called the lake of fire (Rev. 20:14).

Obedience Assignment: ☐

> 36. Envision your campus being transformed into many Disciples for Christ.

All of your student peers are on a path destined for either eternal life with Jesus or eternity away from Him. The plan Jesus has implemented is not to use angels but to use you to inform your student peers about their eternal destiny and bridge your story to how they too can have assurance of eternal life with you.

It requires vision on your part to believe that you can be used to rescue them. Such vision is only possible if you succeed in forsaking your selfishness and choose to obey Jesus' commission to go, make disciples, teach them to obey what you have been taught, and do so with the assurance that Jesus is always with you to encourage and empower you to draw them into the Kingdom (Matt. 28:18-20).

If His commission seems too much for you, that is where your choice to be a visionary kicks in. Where there is no vision, the people perish (Proverbs 29:18).

Obedience Assignment: ☐

5. Brief Discipleship Lesson - Wise Choices:

> 37. Memorize Proverbs 29:18.

Whenever students are faced with an opportunity, an invitation, or desire, they will typically pose the question, is there anything wrong with this? Their assumption is that if something is not wrong, then it must be right. If they have never heard a sermon against it, do not know any Bible verses condemning it, or see that other Christians are involved, their natural tendency is to conclude that it must be OK.

Obedience Assignment: ☐

38. Think about how you determine your choices

Students are inclined to live life on the line. In other words, when they draw a moral boundary line, they tend to live very close to that line. Their behavior stems from their insatiable curiosity about how close they can get to sin without sinning.

- Can I date a non-Christian?
- What type of music can I listen to?
- Is it OK to have a tattoo?
- Is it all right for me to have a beer?
- Which movies are OK for me to see?

You must realize that your choices affect not only you but your close friends as well. You are accountable for your choices. You can enjoy a free and quality life if you make wise choices rather than foolish ones.

You choose how you spend each day. Though others may try to persuade you to follow them, you will choose whom you will follow.

Jesus said, "Follow Me and I'll make you Fishers of Men."

In your case, you should follow Jesus and influence fellow students to follow you. You will become a leader for Christ.

6. Goal Setting:

The final part of Session 6 is to set goals for next week.

There are six goals to be set following this ES meeting: 1) Boldly assume a leadership role with peer students, 2) Prayerfully review your list of students and circle names with which you will share your story, 3) Make some choice changes from foolish to wise, 4) Journal situations you face this week that tempt you to make foolish choices, 5) Pray for the ES group's vision, and 6) Start a list of students interested in joining an ES Discipleship group.

Student Session # 7

Ultimate Authority

Session 7 emphasizes Ultimate Authority. Strange as it seems, your best freedom comes from your obedience to authority. You should now have a well-established and disciplined life of daily Bible study, prayer, and journaling in your secret place. The teacher will appoint one of the students to assist with this session.

1. Opening:

During a brief time of meditation, think of the majesty and magnificence of God. As Creator, He owns everything in the universe. Though we address Him as Heavenly Father, the Bible refers to Him by many names. The Hebrew or Jewish name for the One God is Yahweh which translates into English as Jehovah.

The appointed student will close this part of the ES session in prayer.

2. How Are You Doing Spiritually?

The teacher will choose group members to share how they are doing spiritually.

Do you sense that you are growing spiritually? Explain how you believe you can grow more relationally with Jesus.

You should be accustomed to speaking openly about your spiritual walk with Jesus. The teacher may need to prompt the students by asking questions about their daily times with Jesus in their secret place and of the state of spirituality in their school.

Obedience Assignment: ☐

> 39. How do you rate the spiritual state of your school? 1...............10

Christianity is intended to be an expanding movement of discipleship. If this is not the case for your school, you are being called to start such a movement.

3. Accountability Time:

The teacher will use this time to call on different students to share about the progress they made with their goals during the past week.

1) How have you chosen to take leadership with your fellow students?

2) Share how some of the Students on your list have responded to your story.

3) Tell the group about the students on your list who are interested in joining an ES Discipleship group.

4) Share about your choice to make a wise decision rather than a foolish one.

5) Read or recall from your journal about a situation where you were tempted to make a foolish decision.

6) Recite Proverbs 29:18: "Where There Is No Vision, The People Perish!"

Obedience Assignment: ☐

4. Vision Casting

> 40. Recommend an ES Discipleship course to a different peer student.

The teacher will cast a vision for the group about being authorized by Christ to continue the work He started. It is awesome to realize that Jesus has delegated His authority to you as one of His co-laborers.

If His commission seems too much for you that is where you're authentic faith in His promises must be leaned on. Remember that you can do all things through Christ who strengthens you.

He depended upon some uneducated fishermen and tax collectors to continue His work after He returned to be with your Heavenly Father. Surely, He will be able to depend upon you. Student leadership is taking responsibility when you are sure you have the authority to do so. Jesus declared, "All Authority in heaven and earth has been given to me."

Obedience Assignment: ☐

5. Brief Discipleship Lesson - Ultimate Authority:

> 41. Name people in your community that have authority.

You advance under stages of authority as you mature. As young children, you were under the authority of your parents or guardians. As you entered school, teachers were added to those having authority over you. If you participate in sports, then you should obey coaches that are in your life to help you become good team players. You add more who have authority over you once you are licensed to drive an automobile: police, judges, and if you violate certain laws and are jailed, you have wardens that must be obeyed.

All of these with authority over you are placed in your life by God to prepare you for His ultimate authority. God has called others to have spiritual authority over you: Parents, Pastors, Youth Leaders, spiritual teachers.

If you wish to really enjoy a free life, you will obey those with authority over you. If you fail anywhere along the way, you attempt to chart your course through life alone or independently. This was the initial sin by Eve and Adam. They took the forbidden fruit thinking that they would be like God and able to be independent choosers of what they believed to be right and wrong. Like them, you assume an attitude of not wanting anyone to tell you what to do!

You limit your freedom as you reject those with authority over you. If you end up under a jail warden, you have no freedom at all!

Obedience Assignment: ☐

6. Goal Setting:

42. Visit a local police station. Bake some cookies for them and tell them how you appreciate their service.

The final part of Session 7 is to set goals for next week. There are five specific goals to be set following this meeting: 1) Tell one of your teachers that you appreciate him or her, 2) Speak to your parent or guardian about how you are grateful for them, 3) Ask your parent or guardian to go with you to take some cookies to the police station, 4) If you attend church, let your Pastor or Youth Leader know that you love them, and 5) As part of your prayers this week, thank God that you can trust His authority over you,

Obedience Assignment: ☐

> **43. Memorize Matthew 28:18-20**

Obedience Assignment: ☐

> **44. Share Your Story, bridge and the Gospel with a student peer.**

Example of Your Story: *Since I have come into a relationship with Jesus, He has shown me my purpose in life, made me His brother/sister, and given me eternal life.*

Example of a Bridge to the Gospel: "*I can show you how to <u>know</u> Your Purpose and have Eternal Life!*"

The Gospel: *God loves you so much that He will forgive you of your poor choices, make you a child of His, and give you eternal life if you will trust Him* (have authentic Faith).

Will you trust Him with your life?

Student Session #8

Others First

Session 8 is your final ES class and once it is completed, your group will be recognized as Disciples of Christ that are fishers of men (students).

1. Opening:

During a brief time of meditation, think of the vast expanse of the universe. Our Earth is like a speck of dust floating around in the universe. You are like a speck of dust floating around on a speck of dust in His universe. You are just one of seven billion people, yet He loves you supremely!

The teacher will appoint a student to close this part of the ES session in prayer.

Obedience Assignment: ☐

2. How Are You Doing Spiritually?

> 45. Tell a student friend about the vastness of God's creation.

The teacher will choose group members to tell how they are doing spiritually.

Speak openly about your

spiritual relationship with Jesus. Considering God's majesty and your finiteness, what is your attitude toward Him?

The group members will be guided to discuss the spiritual state of their schools and how they are affected by the school culture. Based on your observations, will your school be better or worse for the next generation?

3. Accountability Time:

The teacher will use this time to call on different students to share about the progress they made with their goals during the past week.

1) How did the teacher respond to your expression of appreciation?
2) Tell the group about your parent's or guardian's reaction to your expression of gratefulness for them. How will you continue showing your gratitude to them?
3) Explain the process you went through to take cookies to the police station. How did those on duty respond? If you recognize the Police officers you met at the station, how will you react to them in the future?
4) Share how you went about telling your spiritual leaders that you love and appreciate them. How did they respond? How do you plan to please them by serving in your school?
5) How do you feel now that you have thanked God for His protective authority over you?
6) Recite Matthew 28:18: Jesus said, "All Authority in Heaven and Earth Has Been Given to Me."

4. Vision Casting:

The teacher will cast a vision for the group about the rewards waiting for you in heaven.

A popular song declares that we can only imagine what heaven is going to be like (*I Can Only Imagine* by MercyMe). We use this song as background to our www. equippingstudents.com website.

Obedience Assignment: ☐

> **46. Listen to the lyrics of *I Can Only Imagine* by Mercyme.**

The deeds you perform in His name will accumulate rewards to be enjoyed for eternity. That is a very long time!

"Look, I am coming soon! My reward is with me, and I will give to each person according to what they have done. I am the Alpha and the Omega, the First and the Last, the Beginning and the End" (Revelation 22:12-13).

Our natural inclination is to store up treasure here on earth but the Bible instructs us to be wise and store up treasure in heaven where it is eternally protected.

Obedience Assignment: ☐

5. Brief Discipleship Lesson - Others First:

> **47. List deeds in your journal that will result in rewards in heaven.**

To prefer others to yourself is counter-cultural. We not only have a selfish nature but our culture encourages

4. Vision Casting:

The teacher will cast a vision for the group about the rewards waiting for you in heaven.

A popular song declares that we can only imagine what heaven is going to be like (*I Can Only Imagine* by MercyMe). We use this song as background to our www.equippingstudents.com website.

Obedience Assignment: ☐

> 46. Listen to the lyrics of *I Can Only Imagine* by Mercyme.

The deeds you perform in His name will accumulate rewards to be enjoyed for eternity. That is a very long time!

"Look, I am coming soon! My reward is with me, and I will give to each person according to what they have done. I am the Alpha and the Omega, the First and the Last, the Beginning and the End" (Revelation 22:12-13).

Our natural inclination is to store up treasure here on earth but the Bible instructs us to be wise and store up treasure in heaven where it is eternally protected.

Obedience Assignment: ☐

5. Brief Discipleship Lesson - Others First:

> 47. List deeds in your journal that will result in rewards in heaven.

To prefer others to yourself is counter-cultural. We not only have a selfish nature but our culture encourages selfishness. Jesus told us that He did not come to be served but to be a servant. He also instructed us to follow Him.

Obedience Assignment: ☐

> 48. Do a kind deed for a fellow student.

You start preferring others first by listening, remembering, asking, and praying.

6. Goal Setting:

The final part of Session 8 is to set goals for next week.

There are six specific goals to be set following the last ES meeting: 1) Let others go ahead of you at lunch, 2) Offer to help a classmate with a tough assignment, 3) Invite another student to sit with you at lunch, 4) Volunteer to help a teacher, 5) Pay special attention to a non-ES student. Listen to what they want to talk about. Pray for them, and 6) memorize Romans 5:8 "God demonstrates His love for us in this: While we were still sinners, Christ died for us".

Obedience Assignment: ☐

> 49. Memorize Romans 5:8.

Completing all eight discipleship sessions and performing your weekly goals will result in a renewed mind and transformation more like Jesus.

Continue the disciplines of daily communion with Jesus in your secret place and continue following Him.

He will be with you as you continue a sustained discipleship movement amongst your fellow students.

Congratulations:

You are now a Disciple of Christ equipped to be a fisher of men (fellow students). He has commissioned you to take the good news (Gospel) to all parts of the world starting in your school and then unto the farthest parts of the world. You can do what God has called and equipped you to do.

Continue sharing your story with fellow students and refer those interested in joining an ES Discipleship group to your ES teacher. Be sure you provide a way to contact them (i.e. phone, email, etc.).

Continue to practice the daily disciplines of Bible study, prayer, and journaling in your secret place.

Remember, He never leaves you. He awaits you daily in your secret place.

About the Authors

John and Dot Overton are a Christian couple married for 64 years. John is a retired NASA engineer, Dot is his faithful helpmate, and Jesus is their Lord.

About the Editor

Will Overton, John and Dot's grandson, is a Baylor University graduate with a Bachelor of Arts degree in Professional Writing.

Printed in the United States
By Bookmasters